DATE DUE

JE 1402			

DEMCO 38-296

GARDEN OF EXILE

Garden of Exile

POEMS

Aleida Rodríguez

▼

Winner of the 1998
Kathryn A. Morton Prize in Poetry
Selected by Marilyn Hacker

Sarabande 〖S〗 Books

LOUISVILLE, KENTUCKY

g Editor
Sarabande Books, Inc.
2234 Dundee Road, Suite 200
Louisville, KY 40205

LIBRARY OF CONGRESS CATALOGING-IN-PUBLICATION DATA

Rodríguez, Aleida. 1953—
Garden of exile : poems / by Aleida Rodríguez.
p.   cm.
ISBN 1-889330-32-9 (cloth : alk. paper). — ISBN 1-889330-33-7
(pbk. : alk. paper)
1. Cuban American women—Poetry. 2. Cuban Americans—Poetry.
3. Lesbians—Poetry.   I. Title.
PS3568.O348764G37   1999
811'.54—dc21   98-51440
CIP

Cover painting: *View from Upstairs*, 1966, by Fairfield Porter. Photo courtesy of Hirschl & Adler Modern.

Manufactured in the United States of America.
This book is printed on acid-free paper.

Sarabande Books is a nonprofit literary organization.

For my mother

♦

ACKNOWLEDGMENTS

Grateful acknowledgment is made to the editors and publishers in whose journals, anthologies, and textbooks some of the poems contained in this collection appeared originally, as follows:

American Voices: Webs of Diversity (Simon & Schuster, 1997): "Lexicon of Exile"

Anthology of Magazine Verse & Yearbook of American Poetry, 1997 edition: "Lexicon of Exile"

Chester H. Jones National Poetry Competition Winners 1984: "Peter on the Run"

Chester H. Jones National Poetry Competition Winners 1988: "Pas Seul"

De Colores: "The Rosario Beach House" (an early version)

Grand Passion: Poets of Los Angeles and Beyond (Red Wind Books, 1995): "My Mother's Art," "My Mother in Two Photographs, among Other Things"

The Kenyon Review: "History," "Landscape"

The Lesbian Review of Books: "Why I Would Rather Be a Painter"

New Millennium Writings: "Plein Air"

ONTHEBUS 14: "Backyard Opera," "Feast of the Epiphany"

Ploughshares: "The First Woman," "Parts of Speech"

Phoebe: "Felling the Tree" (winner of the inaugural Greg Gummer Award in Poetry)

Poetry-in-the-Windows II, Arroyo Arts Collective: "Concierto de Aranjuez," "Jacaranda"

Prairie Schooner: "My Mother in Two Photographs, among Other Things"

The Progressive: "Lexicon of Exile"

Rattle: "The Return," "Cool Acres," "Lexicon of Exile," "Backyard Opera"

Sojurner: "Exile" (under the title "This Here Life")

Southern Poetry Review: "Threshold"

The Spoon River Poetry Review: "Things We Know," "Torch," "Dark Drum," "What the Water Gave Me," "The Invisible Body" (winner of the 1996 Editors' Prize)

The Squaw Review: "The Garden" (in slightly different form)

"The World's Best Poetry, Supplement IV: Minority Poetry of America: "The Rosario Beach House" (in slightly different form)

Thanks to the National Endowment for the Arts for a Creative Writing Fellowship, and to Hedgebrook for a writing residency at a seminal point in the development of the manuscript.

In addition, I would like to express my deepest gratitude to those who have contributed significantly to my life and by extension this book: my parents, Juan José and Paulina; Juney Ahn; Maritza Barreiro; Kathryn Chetkovich; Catherine, Allan, Lily, and Julian Comeau; Elizabeth Cooley; Bernard Cooper; and Jacqueline De Angelis. My heartfelt thanks to Elizabeth Beverly and Leonard Sanazaro, who read the manuscript in early stages and offered both encouragement and many useful suggestions, and to Betsy Amster for her expertise in matters that stump me. Many thanks to the great folks at Sarabande—I couldn't have wished for a better publisher for my first book. And last but certainly not least, I remain indebted to Marilyn Hacker for her kindness and generosity.

TABLE OF CONTENTS

◆

FOREWORD

◆

This is a first book of remarkable range and maturity, which, while revealing its roots, displays the fruit and flower of its branches. The river of Rodríguez's memory is fed by two languages; her perceptions have the acuity of double vision, which is at once the privilege and the scourge of the bilingual and the bicultural writer. The "exile" of which the poet writes is literal: She was sent away from her native Cuba and her mother tongue at the age of nine, an age when a child is already implicated in language. And she was a child who loved language, who spelled words and names backward and forward to unlock their secrets, who had learned to link description and desire. But it is also the fortuitous exile described by Julio Cortázar, cited by Rodríguez herself in an essay: "...our true effectiveness lies in our ability to profit from exile, to take advantage of these sinister fellowships, to extend and enrich our mental horizons so that when at last we can focus on our own realities, we can do so with greater lucidity and effect."

Not all poets are exiles, but some of us, whatever our citizenship, carry within us that sense of at once enduring a profound displacement and of carrying our only homeland along wherever we drop anchor. Many of Rodríguez's poems, and the aesthetic that informs them, remind me irresistibly of that other inhabitant of elsewheres, Elizabeth Bishop. Like Bishop, Rodríguez evokes the strongest emotions through descriptive precision. Like her as well, Rodríguez is equally adept with fixed forms whose containment liberates volatile subject matter, and with the prose poem in which the familiar becomes profoundly strange, and the strange familiar, through the intensity and clarity of the writer's gaze. These stanzas are from a poem called "Ontology," which eventually reaches back into the memory of childhood separation and forward into adult fulfillment:

Fog thinned like steam, and with a shock
Anacapa loomed—bare, mottled.
Arranged nearby on a sharp rock,
a row of glistening cormorants—
a shelf of Chianti bottles—
ignoring the ignorant.

The noisy boat chugged to a stop
beside a steep metal ladder
we had to clamber to the top,
as the cliffs rose barren and sheer.
Gulls wove a fabric of chatter
and the dervish wind spun our hair.

and this is from the sequence called "Little Cuba Stories/*Cuentos de Cuba*":

It usually rains on my birthday. On this one I am given a permanent and stuffed into a frilly pink dress that's stiff and scratchy. Normally I could have gone jumping the balustrades between the houses, but today I am handed down like something on the assembly line at the tomato canning factory until the last step secures me into the back of someone's jeep where by my side the canvas cover hasn't been completely snapped onto the rusty metal and it flaps, flicking drops of water onto my white patent leather shoes, where they bead but roll off whenever the jeep hits a bump.

The poet with double vision is perpetually viewing the landscape behind the landscape, the face of the anima/animus superimposed on the face of the friend/relative/lover; words reveal to her their cognates and connotations. And for the bilingual, the confidences of a dictionary are dubious at best: behind the English word is a Spanish word (or a Greek or Serb, French or Yiddish one) that ostensibly names the same object or idea, but whose roots are in a different soil, whose syllables resound with another music, a divergent history. The child who loved words, who was silenced in her mother tongue, and who became adroit and eloquent in her adopted one, has learned to distrust vocabularies: Manipulated by dictators, inquisitors, censors, words can be the excuse for or the instruments of repression. Rodríguez the poet looks for a renewed innocence and accuracy in the practice of the plastic arts, whose materials are "forgiving as leaves," to whose condition some of her poems, in their deceptive clarity, aspire. But the fascination of words, their perfidy included, continues to operate. A poem called "Parts of Speech" weaves itself across the origins of two common surnames, the poet's own "Rodríguez" and the dedicatee's English (or anglicized) "Miller":

In yours, an arm rotates a round stone over a grinding bed;
in mine, hands materialize to tie scalloping vines onto posts.

Behind our names lie the measured crush of grain,
the transliteration of grapes —

With *Garden of Exile*, Aleida Rodríguez joins Julia Alvarez, Joseph Brodsky, Olga Broumas, Irena Klepfisz, and Charles Simic in that rare company of poets drawing from two languages, two cultures, while they write in English, who enrich the American language in that diversity, at once resistant and receptive, which is its source of strength. But she is also, and primarily, a writer using her own voice as the paintbrush, chisel, engraver's tool, which makes experience and perception clear, new, the more accessible to us in that it is so entirely her own.

—*Marilyn Hacker*

Paradise is not a place but a condition,
a simple being-alive, a drinking straight
from the spring.

—Scott Russell Sanders

LEXICON OF EXILE

Archaeology

I thought at first it was a bullet—
metallic, cylindrical, one end rounded,
the other flat. But once unearthed
from the garden, the little wheel
design of plastic jewels—the color
of watermelon tourmaline or spring grasses
roadside through New Mexico
blurring past the windows—told me
what I'd found, though its identity
eluded me, retreating into guesses
about its color—what was it?—
or how much remained, or whose lips
it had touched before sealing forever.
Because it certainly won't open now,
though I see a seam two-thirds down
its taut little body and twist and twist.
When I wash it in the sink and scrub
off the rust, searching for a name,
its marbled patina looks art-directed:
Evocative little clouds of reddish sienna
burn against a greenish night in the tropics.
You can hear crickets and, farther off,
the timbre of frogs. From the veranda
you intuit blooms pulsing
in the dark. A lava glow smolders
on the opposite hill, the air gravid.
Its weight in your hand, you think
creyón de labios, something ancient
pushed up red from underneath, something
so childish it's perfect: *crayon for the lips*.

Drawing yourself in, inventing yourself
as the world you know erases itself,
words wash over you and you can't help
but think this one's called "Atlantis," say, or "Pompeii."

The First Woman

She was my Sunday school teacher
when I was just seven and eight.
He was the newly hired pastor,

an albino, alarming sight
with his transparent eyelashes
and mouse-pink skin that looked like it

might hurt whenever she caressed
his arm. Since Eva was her name,
to my child's mind it made great sense

that she should fall in love with him.
He was Adán. Before the Fall
and afterward, her invert twin.

And she, Eva, was blonde as well,
though more robust, like Liv Ullmann.
I loved her honey hair, her full

lips; her green eyes a nameless sin.
(Not that I worried all that much —
the church was Presbyterian.)

In Sunday school, her way to teach
us kids to pray was to comment
on all the beauty we could touch

or see in our environment.
My hand was always in the air
to volunteer my sentiment.

Since other kids considered prayer
a chore, the floor was usually mine.
My list of joys left out her hair

but blessed the red hibiscus seen
through the windows while others bowed
their heads. Her heart I schemed to win

with purple prose on meringue clouds.
—For who was Adán, anyway,
I thought, but *nada* spelled backward?

While hers, reversed, called out, *Ave!*
Ave! The lyric of a bird
born and airborne on the same day.

But it was night when I saw her
outside the church for the last time:
yellow light, mosquitoes, summer.

I shaped a barking dog, a fine
but disembodied pair of wings
with my hands. She spoke in hushed tones

to my parents. The next day I would find
myself up north, in a strange house,
without my tongue and almost blind,

there was so much to see. This caused
Cuba, my past, to be eclipsed
in time, but Eva stayed, a loss.

Ave, I learned, meant also this:
Farewell! I haven't seen her since.

Lexicon of Exile

*Animals seem to fill their skins, trees their bark, rivers
their banks, so beautifully, that we cannot help but see in
their wildness a perfect at-homeness.*

—Scott Russell Sanders

There is no way I can crank a dial,
scroll back the scenery,
perch *sinsontes* outside my windows
instead of scrub jays and mockingbirds and linnets.

There is no way the brightly lit film
of childhood's cerulean sky, fat with meringue clouds,
can play out its reel unbroken by the hypnotist's snap:
You will not remember this.

There is no way I can make that Pan American plane
fly backward, halt the tanks of the Cuban revolution,
grow old in Güines, smelling the sour blend of rice and milk
fermenting in a pan by the chicken coop.

There is no way I can pull the harsh tongue
from my mouth, replace it with lambent
turquoise on a white sand palate,
the cluck of coconuts high in the arc of palm trees.

The trees fingering their dresses outside my windows now
are live oak, mock orange, pine, eucalyptus.
Gone are the *ciruelas, naranjas agrias,*
the *mamoncillos* with their crisp green shells
concealing the pink tenderness of lips.

Earth's language is a continuous current,
translating the voices of my early trees along the ground.
I can't afford not to listen.
They find me islanded in Los Angeles,
surrounded by a moat filled with glare,
and deliver a lost dictionary of delight.

A lingual bridge lowers into my backyard,
where the Fuju persimmon beams in late summer
and the fig's gnarled silver limbs become conduits
for all the ants of the world; where the downy woodpecker teletypes
a greeting on the lightpost and the overripe sapotes fall
with a squishy thud; where the lemon, pointillistically studded
with fruit, glows like a celebration; where the loquat drops
yellow vowels and the scrub jays nesting in the lime
chisel them noisily with their hard black beaks
high in the branches, and the red-throated hummingbird—
mistaking me for a flower—suspends just inches from my face,
deciding whether or not to dip into the nectar of my eyes
until I blink, and it sweeps all my questions into the single sky.

Ontology

For Bia and Randy

On my thirty-seventh birthday
the sea was mercury afloat
and the briny fog was dense, gray,
kissing then swallowing the prow.
So, by inches, before the boat
the world was invented—now, now.

Future's entrance grew tangible.
Molecules gained reality,
making the sea amenable
to our immutable approach,
as if our sole ability
to dream had let our boat encroach.

Skimming the surface of water,
the happily named flying fish—
silver wings pinned to a blotter—
were planes on an inverted sky.
We pointed and gawked, astonished
they could trespass so easily.

Fog thinned like steam, and with a shock
Anacapa loomed—bare, mottled.
Arranged nearby on a sharp rock,
a row of glistening cormorants—
a shelf of Chianti bottles—
ignoring the ignorant.

The noisy boat chugged to a stop
beside a steep metal ladder
we had to clamber to the top,
as the cliffs rose barren and sheer.
Gulls wove a fabric of chatter
and the dervish wind spun our hair.

Once our eyes focused, we could see
the scrubby ice plant pocked with nests,
multiplied to infinity.
Large white gulls, red dots on their beaks
like small traffic lights, did their best
to shepherd the wild speckled chicks.

We chose a headland for the cake
and to pop the cork from champagne,
but the wind made it hard to take
a bite not embedded with grit.
Giddy, I ate it all the same —
whipped cream concealing chocolate.

Peering down at a narrow beach —
an archipelago of seals
who sunned and barked — I ached to reach
down and touch those little islands
to see how it would feel
to cradle one in my own hands.

I recalled, as a nine-year-old,
seeing my green island shrinking
far below the airplane window.
Just before I'd played with a goat,

then, propelled by someone's thinking,
I hovered above, wearing my coat.

Past subject of levitation,
I can now will myself to land
for a yearly celebration
on a spot circled by water —
whether a bleak Channel Island
or a San Juan doesn't matter.

On our way back to the mainland
I thought how anticlimactic
it was to travel the same band
of sea, devoid of the enfold-
ing uncertainty — so undramatic,
so flatly familiar, so old.

At a friend's house, I made a show
of a gift — a watercolor
of my hill in bluish shadow —
painted for me by the woman
who later became my lover,
as bright cards were dealt by the sun.

Through the arched doors to her garden,
dangling over the weathered wall,
matilija poppies beckoned
to find them the best simile.
We settled on, after a lull,
origami eggs-over-easy.

On my thirty-seventh birthday
the world was neither map nor boat
but something glimpsed in a doorway —

a scarf from a magician's hat
that before our eyes seems to float
a moment, then is gone like that.

Parts of Speech

For Jane Miller

*Si la uva está hecha de vino, quizá nosotros somos
las palabras que cuentan lo que somos.*
—Eduardo Galeano, *El libro de los abrazos*

It's the mind that marshals everything into neat sequence
in retrospect—subject, verb, predicate—fooling us
into believing words don't dig their tangled roots in us.
But rooting around we uncover evidence—
fanning files, figures strobe into motion:
In yours, an arm rotates a round stone over a grinding bed;
in mine, hands materialize to tie scalloping vines onto posts.

Behind our names lie the measured crush of grain,
the transliteration of grapes—now abstract, as separate from us
as definitions, definitions that, once removed from the body,
flap like flags claiming the moon. Chances are, our ancestors
were never consumed by dependent or independent clauses
but consumed them instead. Yet what happens to hunger
when what we make is not a thing but an idea, the mind levitating
like a frivolous monarch?

Truth is, the vineyards behind the 300-year-old houses
on the Canary Islands appeared first, wordless,
until, years later, the verb *rodrigar*
jumps out of the *Velázquez* to explain them.
The mind, correcting for the continuity error,
splices it behind the houses, earlier,
so that in the story I tell you I cross the ocean,
verb in hand like a suitcase, ready to lift the vines
into sense, into rows that become the sentences

I am speaking to you—you understand, don't you? —
in a kind of dream, with a fidelity to the future,
spoken by the ventriloquist of the heart.

If you believe the soul is born knowing itself,
then that explains why the famous bullfighter
hides behind his mother's skirts and Churchill stutters as a child,
a record already skipping and popping with age.
And if Julio Cortázar lived life backward—"from cynicism
to innocence, from air to egg"—and Rilke imagines us
"not for a moment hedged by the world of time, . . . incessantly
flowing over and over to those who preceded us
and to those who apparently come after us,"
what happens to the grammar that creates us
and whose utterance is apparently dependent on us?

Is this why *Jane* was the first word
I spoke in English, sprawled on the cool tiles of my front porch
in Cuba, a Dick and Jane book spread before us, my playmates
saying *ha-neh* and I confident about its pronunciation?
The mind, snakily syntactical, places the revelations
in future tense, like that childhood party game
where things are hidden in plain sight: It's the context
that obscures them.

Standing now in what passes for now: the doorway
of my house, night a refectory table between eucalyptus trees—
at its head, in diminishing perspective, the past tense
props elbows on the table like a peasant, ravenous.
Closer there gleams a skyline of covered dishes.
Here come the subverting voles of volition,
the picnic ants of anticipation.

15

Rank

OK, so maybe I haven't lived that long, relatively speaking,
even if 42 years ought to have earned me something,
a kind of respect, if not appreciation for my perseverance,
and I feel so distant from my 20-year-old self,
so far from lapel-holding and smart-mouthing,
so much better able to descant exile, language, the sensuality
of memory. So that when I unwittingly blush, kneeled
before the seated 71-year-old Chilean novelist,
not because of reverence, though there's some of that,
but because he's rather deaf, why do I feel like an interloper?
a whiff of something rank? a sin? I ought to confess
to you, O Stranger, now that you've found me here,
I felt my presence soiled something — whatever it was
made the novelist refuse my hand
and hold on to his glass of water.
Was my outfit too coordinated? My lipstick disconcertingly dark?
Did everyone gawk at the deltas fanning alluvially from my
    dank pits?
It occurs to me perhaps it was my urgency, a kind of scurrying
usurpation, that so repelled the exiled novelist,
skilled as he is at detecting coups,
however futile or subterranean.
Afterward, it's all I can do to make it into my house,
crawl into its farthest back reaches, and there —
among scraps of paper bearing cat hair and rain stains,
on a dusty, cluttered shelf speckled with termite crumbs —
I stumble on an old magazine with an article about Robert Frost
and this picture, by Eisenstaedt, of Frost seated
in his Ripton, Vermont, home in 1955, wearing what looks
to be a white (it being a B & W photo), long-sleeved cotton shirt,

ironed creases rising like hackles along the arms, one hand stalled
partway to his mouth or just dismissed there,
his white hair the fine fibers of an artichoke, flying
every which way, full of static electricity,
his furrowed face turned away, bored, or looking
at nothing in particular, letting the camera get its fill of him
instead, clearly someone who's delivered the work already
and is empty, a bowl resting on a table.
And I want to enter that house,
sit there, satisfied, have someone press
my favorite gabardine shirt just before the photo shoot,
to have done something that was — miraculously —
what I had been meant to do.

Concierto de Aranjuez

Vast yellow plain, heat and the meander of memory, incandescent
edge wavering between shadow and light

opens into bright space, the long hot distance vibrating
between us and desire like an empty yellow house

where we'll never live, the unrequited sun reaching for us
so far below, spendthrifts of its attention

even as it flatters us, aimless on this yellow
plain, interminable as a sermon, but—suddenly—olive trees,

gray-green in the distance, hint at moisture,
the mouth of the beloved parting in the shade.

Our pace quickens and a slight swagger loosens our gait,
foreplay originating in embodiment, our own delight

seeking its twin in the beloved,
our mouths small mountain lakes remembering rain,

we are wet with ourselves, and a melodic curve enters
our bloodstream the way the sky releases its blue snake

into water, breaking the hot surface with such deep wetness,
astonishingly blue to the taste,

its edge cold on our parched
tongues, our sweaty necks, our salty faces,

and where time had seemed childhood's summer,
it now rushes with water's

impatience not to preserve narrative but to squander
the moment, an always that seems to bubble from us,

its language loose, emphatic in its surrender,
possession of itself a gift,

now, at the oasis, replacing the plain burning in our eyes
with water, water gazing at sky.

WHY I WOULD RATHER BE A PAINTER

▰▰▰▰▰▰▰◆▰▰▰▰▰▰▰

The most important thing is the quality of love.
Love means paying very close attention
to something and you can only pay close attention to
something because you
can't help doing so.

—Fairfield Porter

My Mother's Art

In my dream, my mother sat on the floor,
painting several small pictures of Los Angeles.
I recognized City Hall, poking up like a giant Rapidograph pen
behind some low yellow buildings
on which the sun burned fiercely.
And the Ambassador Hotel,
its long awnings and withered glamour,
a bluish evening seeping up its faded façade.
The paintings lay around her on the floor
and she was clearly enjoying herself.
I admired them with surprise
for I had never known my mother could paint
at all, never mind so well.
How had I never known this?
That my mother was a great artist?
And that she did it so naturally,
so casually, just sitting there on the floor,
her work, the obvious product of her delight,
all around her?

Peter on the Run

Hi, it's me—I gotta whisper cuz I'm using the phone in an office I delivered to. Boy! I've seen some magnificent *art* today! They've got this new exhibit up at three-three-three South Hope?—you're not going to believe it. There's a bear? made out of nothing but red women's shoes? with all the straps and things sticking out to simulate fur, I guess. And a figure with breakfast on its lap—sitting in a regular chair they got there—made entirely out of toys! *Toys!* And a live horse and a dead horse, both made out of old boards and chicken wire—I tell you, it's *beautiful*. When I first saw the bear I burst out laughing but stopped because the people around started looking at me.

And I saw a *painting*—somewhere else—sort of blurry? of a room with three glass walls. There's a yellow lamp in the room—it's not on but there's some yellow paint doing something on the floor. And *outside* the glass walls there's a view like downtown: these huge rectangles—blue or aqua?—huge, light-absorbing aqua rectangles! It's *breath*taking. And there's a woman looking out? and a man walking toward her? and it suddenly *hit* me how hard it would be to *talk* to someone who is looking *out* on something like that! Well, listen, gotta go now—talk to you later, pal.

Why I Would Rather Be a Painter

We have our disagreements about paint,
the use of words, and which art is the least
corrosive on the heart, which makes the best
amusement ride for pure escape. No taint
of childhood's mess to hold you back with paint,
I say. A tube of Naples yellow rests
apart from cruelty or cliché. No beast
inhabits daubs of thalo green. But hint
at even such a word as *love* and I
am bent, like Sisyphus beneath the stone.
(I'd rather scrub the fungus from the tiles.)
Give me a brush, some pigment, and my eyes —
I'll render what I would have left alone
with words, the peace inside spreading for miles.

Of course, this is provided I could paint,
which is the sort of lie that language tells
and further illustrates the kind of hell
that lurks — a tarry pit — beneath bright sent-
ences. It is that thing, that Sense for Rent
of words that I despise. Dictators dwell
in palaces of words while peasants swill
the backwash of those lies. Time someone went
and told the emperor of words he's nude —
or, better yet, would simply burn his speeches
and force him to take up the brush. This pitch
of mine has dictatorial tones but made
of nobler stuff, I hope, if it teaches
that those who can, do, and those who can't, bitch.

Still Life with Cup

The steam rises from the coffee cup
like someone yawning on a cold night.
From across the room, the artist
studies it, musing about the steam's color
and shape. How they are both absent,
really. Or only momentarily visible.

She thinks these things are visible
to anyone who can mentally enter the cup,
who can withdraw, becoming absent
from the empirical world, into her private night.
She knows it has nothing to do with a knowledge of color
theory or the accident of being born an artist.

She feels frustrated with being an artist,
how all artists wanted only to be visible.
Once she had loved color
and the ache of light glinting off a cup,
but now she wanted it to be forever night,
a place in which all of it—light, color—was absent.

And she wanted all the people to be absent,
too. Especially the Artists.
She wished on them an endless night,
where they would have to struggle to be visible
to themselves first, grasping onto their souls like a cup
and trying to fill it with color.

She pictures it like a drawing for a child to color,
with firm black lines around it but absent

of pigment. Waiting to be filled like a cup.
That's the most important task of the artist,
she thinks, becoming visible
to oneself before facing the final night.

Turning toward the windows she notices night
has fallen, sucking the color
from the room, making everything less visible.
The objects of her life are becoming absent,
and a shiver runs through the artist
as she tries to focus on the disappearing cup.

In a panic to be visible, she holds up her absent
hand, but it is in night's mouth, along with all the color.
Is she the artist, or the cold cup?

Still Life with Glass

After Janet Fish

...like gardens poured in glass, clear, unattainable.
—Rainer Maria Rilke

On the green marble table
(green as a moment
deep within a forest,
branches twisting, brook
wending crookedly through it)
the glass of water glows
pale green and suspends
an undulating forest
in its sling of liquid.
The scene is sealed
with a meniscus of mercury:
a mirror in a fairy tale.

Still Life: *June 16, 1987*, Oil on Board

For A.

At the seaside cottage
the family is lulled by the infinity of the mundane.
On the porch facing the beach
the daughter, a painter, rearranges the china from breakfast:
a stack of yellow plates soft as pancakes pooling amber syrup,
the pitcher with its milky lip, cups turned in conversation,
their white mouths addressing the contemplative sugar bowl,
the coffeepot gesturing out to sea,
the gravy boat curled catlike on its yellow rug.
Anchoring the center, a green-glass vase
gently branches a nervous system of baby's breath into the air.

Beyond the wooden porch frame
the sea blurs and grays like memory,
and tiny pink bodies poke up from the sand.
One of them, to the right of the vase, is her father fishing.
She pauses and squints at him. Distant,
he is the size of her hand, and she recalls another beach picture:
her body so small it nestled between his crouched legs,
her arm thrown casually around his neck.
That moment as permanent as a constellation.

The blue grid of the tablecloth buoys up the brilliant dishes,
glowing from within like treasure in the cave of a fairy tale.
With luminous eyes she composes
the remnants of breakfast into a family portrait.
She delights in the way the golden glaze
mutates with the angle of the sun.

There is love in her eye, turned on the everyday,
and she laps up the light like syrup.

Then a storm rushes in with a dark crackle,
a candle extinguished with wet fingertips.
She notes the specific shade of navy blue
the sky turns, a blotter soaking up spilled ink.
Figures rise from the water and run toward the house.
The air is charged, a half-moon of stillness trapped under a cup.
The entire family assembles on the porch,
waiting for the heavy curtain to rise.
It is the father who's the actor,
marching up and down the pier, gathering beached belongings.
As he grabs an aluminum chair,
the heavens reach down to take his last picture.

When the daughter arrives by his side, his eyes are startled—
like hers, but with another vision.
The flash has rendered his pupils tiny as pinpricks on a blue field.
On the wet boards he resembles the fish he caught that day,
and she knows her father is not there.
The sky rips open, reuniting the sea with its twin.

At the hospital
the family paces around the empty room that used to be the father.
It is impossibly blue and gold again,
so quick was this night cupping day. Capricious
as a bored child toying with ants under a teacup.

Gradually the pattern emerges, a net
bringing up clues from the mirror-world below:
the father's contest with nature,
the daughter's childhood song
joining them like a wraith in the restaurant,

his closing remarks, his impatience
to pack up the car and leave.

Landscape

At home it is a Dutch landscape:
The houses terraced on the hills are bathed in golden light
as though viewed through aged varnish. They are nestled
into the soft, grassy slope like ornaments on green frosting.
The scene is framed in my rearview mirror
as I descend onto the freeway.
Midroad it's instant night,
a panorama of grays and deeper grays.
The wet sheet of rain blows up and sticks against the windshield.
The headlights of other cars are buttery yellow roses
losing their petals on the glassy pavement.
The dark curtain of asphalt is thrown aside briefly
and our world is suddenly revealed to us:
standing on bright stilts above a chasm.
The car is striped with wavy rivulets. They wriggle and crawl
toward me like all the tears I wasted on futile things
coming back, crawling back, wriggling back.
I stop for bread, eggs, maple syrup, cheese, mineral water.
The paper bags wilt in the rain as I run back to the car.
It is 3 p.m. but it might as well be 8.
I merge back into the dark river.
Midroad it's brilliant again: Warm yellow light
seeps around gray-bottomed clouds, so many fat biscuits
rising on a pale blue cookie sheet.
The hills are as green as the piece of felt I cut out
in elementary school.
Why is felt always in past tense?
I could reach out the window now
and touch those hills with my giant fingertip.
Back at home, no clouds overhead,

just a transparent blue bowl turned upside down.
And there it is again, that Dutch landscape, unchanged,
as though I'm passing it once more in a gallery.
But the shadows are now a bit greener, the houses slightly pinker.
Inside, my lover is still leaning into her easel, squinting,
pushing her brush into a street in her hometown,
three thousand miles away.
Tiny gnats are trapped in the smoky cobwebs on the ceiling.
I am standing in the doorway,
but all of this is already in the past.

Plein Air

I'd like to explain
how difficult it is to work with words.
A painter sits down and lines up
little tubes of color cleansed of context.
The autistic tubes in a row
utter nary a sentence, don't waggle
with admonishment or squirm with shame.
There's no fear their tiny silver mouths
will whisper *fucking mustache* or *fat immigrant,*
you never or *I always* or *don't.*
No one has hissed cadmium yellow
in a fit of rage or spat chrome oxide green
while walking out the door.
Free from these radioactive insinuations,
the painter can open up the top of her head,
release the words blackening its ceiling
like trapped smoke and go to work
with the vocabulary of another planet.
Her materials are as forgiving as leaves,
which care not whether she says
detergent instead of *iconoclast.*
When she opens up the case,
the colors are all there exactly
as she left them, not dangling
between her and the checkout clerk.
They're pristine, untroubled,
idiot savants with an amnesiac's satin memory.
She doesn't have to autoclave
each one before she picks it up.
There should be such a box for writers,

filled with words brightly minted
but spared the smudge of circulation,
words denied to cruel, rapacious partners,
jealous coworkers, spin doctors, and ad copywriters.
Words one could pick up and squeeze
a little bit of on a palette, add
a splotch of medium and swirl
to just the right syrupy consistency.
Thus preserved, these words would sweep
the mind free of muddle, the sky of pollution,
and, virginal as illustrations in social studies books
before we understood the West was actually lost,
blue-creased mountains would loom, crisply visible,
their presence saying simply *winter,* saying *late afternoon,*
saying *here.*

DARK DRUM

Things We Know

Not only that she played with her lip while reading,
or that I sleep with my hands curled up like baby animals.

Or things told with fingers still sticky from sex, late at night,
the bed an island from which we hoped never to be rescued.

Told like constructing a mosaic, each detail a shard of color
slowly and deliberately placed until the picture breathes:

A face shines down, moist, released from the telling but wary.
What will you do with this information?

It's tempting to be the exception—*no one before understood you
like I can*—and with that the bed dislodges from the dusty
    floorboards,

scattering tumbleweeds of dog hair, and we're off.
But we've signed on to a cruise with a stranger, a perfect stranger,

who only through the daily gospel of bathroom habits
is revealed as the Flawed Being—in a tattered bathrobe—

we have always loved. Or at least we hope so. Too often, years
down the line, we turn to make a casual comment and confront

instead the face of childhood's scowling monster—which is to say,
after a while we know a thing or two about each other.

And sometimes, unlike the first tender glimpse behind the curtain,
it's not a gift, though it rushes, breathlessly, toward us.

Pas Seul

The room is dark green, a cool green vault, darkness deep within woods. The two windows are shuttered with mahogany blinds against the scorching light. Paintings—small far-off views, relics of the world outside—offer the only visual exits. Naked on the bed, I am the only thing conducting heat. My body is steaming, leaving a someone-died-here outline on the sheets. Sweat gathers in droplets and cascades from my underarm hair, little waterfalls pouring spots like ink when you pause pen to paper while thinking. I'm letting go of thinking to receive images on the screen of my body. When the room disappears, the good ones arrive, flickering along the fiber optics of memory: that favored hillock of ass, an aerial view of breast like custard sunk back into its cup with tiny parenthetical ripples, the nipple firm and rising mesalike, a tongue roving in long swathes like someone licking a bowl of frosting. Marshy, I am almost absorbed by the mattress. The arch of my lower back is a brazier of coals. The yellow ceiling lifts and recedes. When I drop spiraling like Dorothy's house, my head lolls heavily on the pillow. Through the open door, the shoes in the closet are a chorus of Ohs and Ahs.

Cool Acres

This emptiness is normal, the richness
of our own neighborhood is the exception.
          —*Powers of Ten*, Charles and Ray Eames

Like sculpture: her friends, her cats, her parrot.
She knew the dream meant we all die alone,
the dead's description of it as "Cool Acres"
wasn't so beveled as to be impossible to see through:
acres and acres of rolling green land dotted with picnic tables
under shady trees, one tiny frozen-custard stand,
all the picnickers gone.

When she rearranges her hair or brushes her teeth,
she notices things passing behind her that aren't there
when she turns. The windows of her house
are emitting and receiving messages. She wonders
who is talking about her, what dead relative is bored
and making crank calls, what piece of the future
has become dislodged and is floating backward
to meet her ahead of schedule.

A red-throated hummingbird pokes among the loquat blooms.

History

*In art, politics, school, church, business, love
or marriage — in a piece of work or in a career —
strongly spent is synonymous with kept.*

—Robert Frost

She taught me the names of flowers: calendula, ranunculus, Iceland poppy. And the medicinal uses of herbs: Fenugreek opens up a stuffy head; goldenseal lubricates the cracked mucous membranes. Over a circa 1820 American dropleaf table, she told me asparagus was the broom of the kidneys. I hadn't understood at first and thought she'd used a German word I pictured as *brüm* and not as the little stalks standing on their heads, sweeping out the impurities. I learned to make the perfect roux for soufflé and became her efficient assistant in the kitchen — dicing and chopping, she once told me, with unparalleled patience. Then one day she began to accidentally break my Depression glassware, and I recalled how she'd giggled when she told me that in two years of marriage she had single-handedly decimated her husband's glass collection dating from 1790 to 1810, including a rare wedding goblet. In the doorway to the back porch she stated simply that my presence made her feel strangled, it was nothing I was doing or could do. We saw a therapist for six years, while my collection dwindled then became memory. With unparalleled patience I jumped through hoop after burning hoop, the therapist pointed out, but I heard that as praise for my prowess and continued to balance Bauer plates on my nose on command; hold growling tigers off with Windsor dining room chairs; juggle career, job, hope, and nightly tempests with unparalleled dexterity. I could reassemble anything: shattered pictures of us crossing the street with canes in the future, my hand under her elbow. My heart. But what I lacked, I can see now, was the ability to dissemble. Finally, she brought home a Cuisinart food processor, and I started hearing the minutes slicing away with ferocious velocity, time doing its soft-shoe faster and faster like Fred Astaire on amphetamines. Memories of flowers and herbs were sacrificed to the angry god of its vortex. Your voice is like acid on my skin, she said after twelve years, then grabbed her Cuisinart and left me behind like so much history.

Descent

Two years ago the sun drove its wavy red spears
into the earth, and inside houses
candles abandoned their upright shapes,
dreaming the liquid sleep of snakes.
Two years ago the heat waves spoke to you,
insinuating a sinister frequency into your brain.

The watery blue grid that lies submerged,
ordering our lives,
sizzled for you like electrical entrails —
a toaster's red net catching you in its scheme.
The only thing to do
was to join the dog under the car
where the soiled underbelly of the world
presented itself, an equation on chalkboard.

Later that day the restaurant's red wallpaper
made you wonder why everyone was so angry
and your stomach tensed: You couldn't eat a thing.
The red snapper's fried skin crackled static.
The waiters conspired in a foreign tongue.
You spoke in verse, the cadence of tragedies.

Today you alternate between
your sweltering garage studio
and the cool dark workroom at the center of the house
like someone carrying buckets of water to a fire.
Today your paintings are twilight windows
opening on the ordinary
at the precise instant when the extraordinary

crosses over into this world, spirit seeking shape.
As you labor toward the source,
buckets clanging against your thighs,
night deepens into the obscure blue tunnel of descent,
and day searches for its fiery face
over the dark wall
on the glassy surface
at the bottom of the well.

Torch

Light from a dead star—even at the beginning,
her phone messages sounded like that to you,
her voice snappy as women in thirties films:
the wisecracking gun moll with a heart of gold.
Red gowns in windows made you think of her,
bare shoulders evanescent as dreams for the future.
In her apartment, cigarette smoke monogrammed the air,
wafted like strands of hair into her eyes
when she leaned forward or cocked her head, whiskey in hand.
Then the late-night revelations: childhood
leg braces, the reason for the coquettish way
she stands with one leg crossed over the other.
You love this, being let in behind the curtain,
but then there you are, of course—
you hadn't expected to be pulled into this,
one minute watching comfortably from your seat,
the next, stirring risotto at the stove,
tension rising like granite in your shoulders.
When you turn you hope to god
your flushed cheeks can be blamed on the flame
or the wine. The floor, sinking beneath you,
no longer your lousy linoleum.
You sputter, try to cut angles into your voice,
sharp crags to pull yourself out with—
things like *dame* and *swell* and *packin' heat*—
but, face it, she's running the show.
You feel suddenly weak, like you might drop
to your knees right there in the kitchen
and propose. Is this really you, with the moon
in your eyes? The corny words to torch songs

in your head? Dinah Washington
crooning, *If I were a salad I'd be splashin' my dressing.*
If I were a goose I'd be cooked....

Rimas Dissolutas

The mock orange tree, asparagus fern,
and royal palm on this side of the hill
yield their green to dusk, payment
for entering the funhouse of night.
Across the ravine, shadow laps
halfway up the slope, where pastel houses
still perch on the shore of day,
incandescent lovers beaming
for a snapshot. The only darkness they know
yet is a treetop's silhouette,
the head of the future
cast back across this scene.

Watching from here, I don't know what to mourn,
or even if I should—doesn't everything fall
eventually? Rome, apples, the accident
of love? The palpitation at first sight
eventually down-curves off the map.
(At this, dry leaves scrape a wry applause
along the drive.) Now the definite shapes
of things are novocained by night. The tunneling
beams of cars look like snowplows
of the underworld pushing dark drifts out—
then down. Something used to be there,
but now it's money in a dream.

Eclipse

When it's the moon, it's an icy grin,
a wink, a random
falling eye-
lash.
Solar,
you
must
not
use
the
naked
eye, but
let it pass
onto paper, where it
documents silent armies advancing against
a tiny country, its citizens massed brightly at the border.

Dark Drum

For K.

The deep night you lured me
away from sleep into fragrant coolness
frogs resonated the air
with sonorous cello suites.

When invisible deer galloped
just ahead of us, our hearts
our hearts leaped up, hooves echoing
on the dark drum of earth.

Were we afraid
they were charging toward us
or finally escaping
the secret corral of our ribs?

50

Threshold

It is I who misunderstood everything and let everyone down....
I am still running, running from that knowledge, that eye,
that love from which there is no refuge.
                    —Annie Dillard, "God in the Doorway"

I emerge from under the cool oaks, follow a path
grooved into a sunlit field sloping gently upward, splashed
with low shrubs and singular, thin-stemmed blooms
I add to the list of what I do not know.
Gnats effervesce above and a breeze reveals the grasses
waving slim batons, shaking their shaggy,
passionate heads full of music. Here and there, bronze grasses
hurl themselves down, reaching in the same direction,
like the arms of lovers longing toward an absence.
But this is only human failing—
grasses having no regrets, love and death and life
being one to them, not separated into before and after.

A scrub jay rends the air with its rusty-hinged call
like the screen door screeching open last night.
In the half-light of an oil lamp I heard the shrill squeal
and my eyes locked on the threshold of what I know,
my rigid body a door closed against it.
And when I called out *Hello?...Hello!*
—not so much a greeting as a shield of sound—
whatever it was let go of the door, let it clap like a heavy lid,
releasing the handle to my world, knowing my hello
was proprietary, a No Trespassing sign
hung on the barbed wire of language.

And when the rusty jaw shut on something left unsaid,
there remained the echo of my hello, empty, meaning instead,

Whoever you are, I'm not ready for you, not ready
to marry my fear to your bright love, dissolving my words
to mist, words I have built into a cabin in the woods.
And I regretted my reluctance,
masked as bravery, passing for self-possession—
for what had I mistaken I possess?
Who had I turned away at the door?

CUENTOS DE CUBA

The Rosario Beach House

1.

al amanecer   el monstruo del mar dormía
and the sea licked at the edge
with flat tongues of mercury   quiet and slow
después de leche con café
y pan con mantequilla   mi abuela and I
went into the water   antes que los otros
she walked easily in the ocean   caminaba
conmigo en sus brazos   the sound of her large legs
parting the water   the legs that later I see
in the sun with sea salt drying white
on her skin   cruzada
con ríos rojos y azules
in her black bathing suit

ella en su gordura   floated in the water
como un globo o una ballena   I liked
her way without fear   no como mi mamá
who has always feared water in such abundance
the bathwater, no   ni la de lavar las ropas
en el patio   but the ocean, yes
that was one thing out of her influence
but over the sandbars caminaba
su madre   carrying me
to what seemed to be the end of the ocean
my arms around her neck
sometimes the water would reach my back
a veces más baja   but always warm
and so clear   que mirando para abajo

I could see the strong feet of mi abuela
on the white sand   firmes
en agua como si en la tierra

2.

the middle part of the day
I spent con los niños de los vecinos
or others who came to visit   el día
siempre era pasado en chores
y chancletas de goma   running
after the melcocha vendor
who passed dressed in white for the heat
with those long, pointed candies
the color of azúcar quemada
or following a straight line
along the water until we reached
la parte más remota de la playa
more sand than houses
las casas misteriosas
we imagined brujas or locos
lived in them
out here   so far

3.

la regularidad de esos días
was broken once a week   when mi tío Guicho
came to take me   a la ciudad
para mis inyecciones   in his '46 dust-covered
Chevrolet that was really black underneath

por el camino pasábamos fincas
fields cupping water   I didn't understand
mi tío Guicho said: es bueno para el arroz
arroz
arroz
erre con erre cigarro
erre con erre barril
rápido corren los carros
por la línea del ferrocarril
I chanted quietly until we reached the clinic
where I extended the same arm each time

al regresar   muchas millas de la playa
I stuck my head out the window
I knew I was the one who could
smell it farthest away
yo decía: puedo oler el mar

there were three long folds of skin
on either side of his mouth
when mi tío Guicho laughed

4.

por la tarde
nosotros y los vecinos   drifted
out of our houses to fish
todos nos sentábamos a la orilla
on large barnacled posts nailed to the edge
with ladders reaching to the water
our padres or abuelos   smoking
their tabacos to one side of their mouths

la gradual caída del sol
made us swallow our words
as if we were the ones swallowing the sun
a veces uno u otro gritaba   feeling
the rod slip in his hand
los niños corríamos a ver
to see the media luna that had been caught
always the same   all of them with eyes that never closed

without speaking   nosotros, los niños
drew our feet from the water
as long rectangles of light stretched
from the houses across the gravel road
and to our backs   we knew
that water could swallow you
into nightmares now   it was the place
out of where night rose and was absorbed
into the air   era la hora
cuando no se podía confiar en el mar
o en las cosas familiares del día

we made the world smaller
and brought it inside in our buckets
with the blue-and-silver fish
we fried in manteca
until the eyes turned white
like the nieve we had never seen

5.

the house trembled with my coughs
y los respiros de mis fantasmas de noche

Little Cuba Stories/*Cuentos de Cuba*

I.

The house is long like a boxcar. It anchors down a corner of *el solar*, an apron of field spreading off to the left, which is further held down by pig troughs and pigs, horses and their thatch shelters, red-white-yellow chickens and roosters, a goat, and a cow. The fence is wire and all the animals and the man tossing out a bucket of yellow/orange corn can be seen clearly. Behind the house, piles of windshields and fenders and bumpers glint and sway in the heat.

The boxcar house has a short picket fence skirting its front yard, some years painted white, others blue. There are violet margaritas along the right side of the path up to the porch, and centered on the left side, the naranja agria tree with its skinny, whitewashed trunk. The small porch has a concrete balustrade dividing it from the six other porches extending to the right, each one bracketed by its own low balustrade, like hurdles.

> It usually rains on my birthday. On this one I am given a permanent and stuffed into a frilly pink dress that's stiff and scratchy. Normally I could have gone jumping the balustrades between the houses, but today I am handed down like something on the assembly line at the tomato canning factory until the last step secures me into the back of someone's jeep where by my side the canvas cover hasn't been completely snapped onto the rusty metal and it flaps, flicking drops of water onto my white patent leather shoes, where they bead but roll off whenever the jeep hits a bump.

At the photographer's I sit on bright green straw with my dress like a pink fan, one knee crossed over the other, my hands cupping the top knee. Later he adds extra red to my cheeks, more pink to the starched bows pinned to my hair—my temples ache with the pull. He touches up my teeth, too. They've never been good.

Little Cuba Stories/*Cuentos de Cuba*

II.

Opening the door of the house at one end lets you see all the way to the half-cemented backyard. The path is so direct and without obstacle that the small dog my sister and I brought home sees the front door open from the backyard, streaks through the house, escapes—and is later found eating and rolling around happily in the rotting carcasses by the slaughterhouse. That's the way she dies. The men poison the discarded meat. They were tired of her frequent visits. But not until I am safely in this country, spared the spectacle my father saw before he buries her.

Little Cuba Stories/*Cuentos de Cuba*

III.

The floor is tiled, green with gray swirls. A piano stands against the left wall, facing a couple of caned chairs that raise perfect little circles on my thighs when I sit for too long in shorts. Always on the wall between this, the living room, and the arched doorway to my parents' room is a wall vase shaped like a long triangle and being, in its own reality, the body of Mary covered in robes with gold rays painted onto the ceramic space surrounding her. She is only the front of the vase. The back is hollow to hold water, and I can see the contours of her body from the inside when refilling it.

Looking closely at the corners of the room, you can see a yellowish stain, as though the house had at one time been submerged during a flood that lasted many years. But the reality is that my father smokes large black cigars and spits wherever he pleases, and he pleases especially in the corners of this room. In one corner sits the black-and-white television on a small wooden table. Or, years before, the cardboard box we cut TV-size, put tissue paper for the screen, glued on characters cut out of the comics, and moved a candle in back to make them dance.

Little Cuba Stories/*Cuentos de Cuba*

IV.

There are two entrances to my parents' room: one arc by the TV and the one that shoots straight through the house. It is in this room, where the bed looms like a whale, that I receive last-minute primpings from my mother. I stand in front of her while she holds my chin tight to make sure I won't turn my face away as she powders me, getting it in my nostrils and eyes.

Little Cuba Stories/*Cuentos de Cuba*

V.

A.

There are no doors between the rooms. The archways bore through the house like a tunnel through a mountain. The room one falls into after my parents' is the largest and serves as two bedrooms divided by an invisible wall. Half of it is my brother's and the other half my sister and I share, but not at first.

Earlier, I have a bed to myself on the side of the room nearest the kitchen. My bed is low and on one side a wooden rail can be dragged up noisily and clicked into place.

> It is here my little goat wakes me, grabbing the covers off me with her teeth. We play in the empty pig shelter at the far end of the patio while my mother washes clothes in a *palangana* and throws the soapy water across the concrete, where it steams.

> But my father is a butcher by profession, and my family has other plans for my goat: a Sunday picnic at the zoo in Havana. The day is huge and blue and breezy. My sister teases me for not eating and says my goat is delicious. I stray away to watch the monkeys.

> I give one of the monkeys near the fence my banana. As it finishes peeling it meticulously, another monkey appears behind it and shoves the banana into its own mouth. The first monkey turns around, slaps it in the face with the

empty peel, but that monkey isn't sorry and starts jumping and screeching and showing its yellow teeth.

For many years, those monkeys are all I can remember about the picnic at the zoo.

B.

Later, when my sister and I share a bed on the other side of the room, I can see the tall narrow cabinet right inside my parents' room. My father always puts his hat on top of it as he walks in. And at night, through the mosquito netting, it is a tall thin man wearing a straw hat, lurking just outside the door, watching me in a sinister way. The dead weight of my sister's habitual leg thrown across my body is no talisman. I have to keep waking myself up, sweaty and tense, to make sure he hasn't moved any closer.

My Mother in Two Photographs, among Other Things

There she is, standing next to her own mother, behind the symmetrical and somewhat religious arrangement of two Coca-Cola bottles flanking a birthday cake on a small table. If you look closely, it's really the sewing machine shut down, the cake on the slightly raised platform in the center, where the machine part turns upside down into its cabinet: a little altar for an impromptu picture of "just the family."

It is December 1962, my cousin María's eighth birthday. My brother, my sister, and I were sent five months earlier to a foreign country, so we are not in the picture. In two days, my grandmother will die, and on the right side of the photograph, directly opposite her, forming a Rorschach double, lurks the dark figure of the guide who came to lead her away. The shadow's hand is on its hip, its face swirls in a smoke that obscures the features. My grandmother is the only one not looking—even the baby held up by Panchito is—into the camera, the eye of the future. She seems distracted, as though she's contemplating an answer. Two days after her party, María and Panchito wake up with our grandmother, who has wet the bed and will not rouse.   .

But what about my mother? Like opposite aspects of the same person: my mother, my grandmother's shadow. Here, she's smiling, though not broadly. Her children are gone, but her mother's there, telling her *aguántate, cálmate,* as they sit over *café.* Or maybe she's relieved. It is, after all, the first time since their marriage that she and my father are alone, like newlyweds. But suddenly a kitchen towel, embroidered with the day of the week, *martes,* and smeared with another woman's lipstick, flies from my mother's hand, lands like an open book by my father's mud-caked boots.

In this photograph, a coffee-dark V shows through the collar of her dress, evidence of the enforced labor in the cane fields since the revolution. Above her head is a wall vase filled with plastic flowers, hanging under the framed painting of a saint, who can't be seen above the melted-chocolate folds of a robe, and above that, perhaps, two hands are held palms up, checking the spiritual weather. But the hands are outside the photograph, just like my hands, which can't touch my mother at that brief oasis, or my grandmother, right before she turned and left with the shadow.

Grandmother left so abruptly, left my mother in midsentence, fingering the legendary length of fabric her mother had once transformed into the Miracle of the Three Dresses. Alone, she collapsed into her mother's absence like a slave into bed at the end of the day.

Then one afternoon two years later the air of her kitchen spun like someone whirling toward her, and she knew something had happened to her son: locked in a mental ward at sixteen after chasing his foster mother around the block with a kitchen knife. He had dropped out of high school, washed dishes for a living. Sporting long sideburns, he rewarded himself first with a round-backed two-toned Chevy, then a series of garish Mustangs. Married to his fate, he left a trail of cars, each wrapped like a wedding ring around a telephone pole.

A vision of her oldest daughter—forever regretting she hadn't been born into a TV family—flashed thin against the white walls of college, her body a blade sharpened to sever the question from the answer. Her face a glossy ad of the ideal American living room.

In the newspaper photo above the caption "Family of Cuban Expatriates Reunited Here," I am the only one gazing at the camera, my face twisted into a complex curiosity. Two years on my own among strangers had only taught me how to be one. I stood, my first tongue ripped out, with my mother's wet, round cheek pressed to the top of my head. The dark flag of her mustache. Their sour smell, like clothes trapped in a hamper. Emblems of the exile. While bureaucrats toyed with their time and their fate, my parents had waited, uncomplaining, afraid.

But I didn't know that back then. I placed myself instead in the camera lens, looking back at the spectacle we made in the bus station. Under my skin, the rice fields of my hometown were flooding the place of language. Though my mother pulled me toward her with one arm, she scooped up only watery absence; my body had long since drifted downriver. My mother's face in this photograph, captured by a stranger, betrays the weight of emptiness in her arms.

Felling the Tree

In the morning Kique and my father come to cut down
the Japanese evergreen pear tree. Kique, eighty years old,
little and bowlegged like a whittled caricature,
climbs the tree, begins sawing off the topmost branches.
My father, nearly seventy-nine, tall and slender
but for his spider belly,
stands on the driveway, looks up at Kique and says,
An eighty-year-old man climbing trees!
in the derisive voice he uses affectionately when he's outdone.

The tree is six times Kique's height, but he brings it crashing down
limb by limb as though dismembering the idea of old age.
Then he toddles on the ground, his two-foot machete singing
the thin branches off. He says the machete is so good
because it's Kique's brand—and doesn't bother to explain.
He says the same thing about the saw and clippers he uses to reduce
the mess into neat bundles he carries on his head, dumps by the curb.

Unraveling stories of other trees, Kique's mouth
is connected to the decisive movement of his arms and legs.
He looks like what Geppetto might have created,
thinking of a Cuban cowboy.
His voice is rough and high, as though he survived a horse's kick.
He won't come into my house, so he pees by the garage.
My father watches and listens, the tip of his tongue bitten down
at the corner of his mouth, the way he used to do with cigars
before the doctor told him he had to quit.
This is not his territory,
but he saunters over to hold one end of the trunk
Kique is rendering into logs with his chain saw.

My father daintily throws thin branches
across the lengths of cord Kique has cut for bundling.
He does this hesitantly, a sculptor
waiting for the muse to guide his hand.

The whitefly infestation from the felled tree hovers
like arrested snow flurries,
or like the snow on a TV screen after the last show.
Or what memory will do to the events of this morning,
once these two have packed up the tools and walked,
congratulating themselves on their little victory,
down the long driveway and into the flickering distance.

Exile

It's like in your chest there's a magnet, a magnet not for metal but for a substance not available on this planet. So that it is constantly pulling—angular little shocks like in the cartoons—at something it will never draw close. Must be where they got the expression *aching for something*. Because it is a kind of ache. To want something and want something and. After a while you begin to feel intimate with the missing part. You begin to feel it's natural not to feel pleased or satisfied. You look for houses in dead ends to live in.

And the heart keeps pace with it. You begin to miss everything. All things past. You begin to feel as though you finally caught up with them all: the perfume of night within a particular season, the cardinal's call from the tree by your window in an old house. You put words to the tune: *I want so much, I want so much, I want, I want, I want, I want.* A familiar neighborhood and how it felt to walk the streets down their middles because it is so early no cars are out. Views—of things, from things.

All those times that almost did it for you are here now for your birthday, crowding their pointed faces around you for the photograph. You invite them onto the train—the same train you've been on as you've seen them pass by. You help them with the small bags they carry, grabbing some by their elbows to steady them up the steps. But you stay on the platform and wave to them this time. The train's windows are all busy with the colors they're wearing. You wave and wave in order not to let them know.

THE GARDEN

Feast of the Epiphany

The infusion of evening is steeping
in the last golden liquid of day,
submerging the backyard in a lavender greenness
where only my neighbor's oranges glow
over the back fence, clinging to the light
and storing it within themselves.
I'm listening to the Fourth Movement of Mahler's Fifth,
holding a tiny glass of amontillado.
Suddenly I remember today
is January 6, the Feast of the Epiphany,
the day three wise men finally
reached the manger to witness the glow
curled within the sleeping child
and felt a sweetness strummed
like a harp within their breast.
Did they also feel a heaviness pulling at them,
the way we feel something materializing
behind the door of our joy,
ready to knock,
maybe not today, so sweet and amber,
but soon?

The Gravelly Path to the Woodpile

First morning in the cabin: barely daybreak,
a small metallic sound—*pik-ping, pik-ping, pik-ping*—
the Tin Woodman's new heart. I listen, eyes closed.

♦

Next morning, the sky a gray flannel pulled over dawn,
it comes again—children chucking pebbles at my car?
No children here, I remind myself.

♦

Third day, nothing miraculous—
just a brown towhee pecking at my car's chrome hubcaps.
Crazy bird's going to give itself a concussion,

and I move closer, thinking to help, but he skitters off,
watches me from a brittlebrush, his mad eye a funnel of focus.
As I turn my back, he starts again: *pik-ping!*

Insolent, disobedient, stubborn child.
Go ahead, I scold, *crack your head open, see if I care.*
And close my door.

♦

Every morning at the rim of day
I wake, convinced it is the middle of the night,
and stare, unrested, into the dark bowl of the valley.

Then my eyes discern a rosy pulse, a fertile egg held up to light.
And lo! — 'tis not the nightingale,
it is the Towhee, Herald of the Morn.

♦

Pik-ping! pik-ping! I begin to speculate, watching termites
migrating like herds of winged buffalo across the ceiling:
Could it be aggression? Another bird

the towhee thinks he sees,
so impertinent as to confront and taunt him
on his own territory?

♦

The full moon lowers itself into an azure bath, and I translate,
slowly, like someone untangling the syntax of a foreign tongue:
Perhaps it is his love he sees, so near, yet trapped

behind the veil of an invisible spell, as in a fairy tale.
Why does he persist? Is his skull too tiny
to let in something as big as the impossible?

I get up, feed wood into the stove, move away
from such thoughts and wade into my useful day,
now a pool of yellow light.

♦

Then today, head full of nothing but the gravelly path
to the woodpile, I come upon him, not just pecking
but flinging himself, breast first, against the silver bubble,

his needlelike claws screeching faintly
against his reflection as he slides off,
again and again, obsessed.

—No, faithful. Every morning we rise.
The horizon—mountains filed behind one another in descending
    shades of gray—
becomes visible and pulls away, leaving us.

Yet we rise, hurl ourselves against the image
of this world, wanting to pierce it, to comprehend,
wanting to be let in.

The Return

I open the door and someone flicks a switch:
Surprise! The alder saplings shimmer like waterfalls.
A bug—long and sleek as a black canoe—
climbs and climbs the green waves under my toes.

The bees had been impatient for me to come out,
tapping against my windows like lovers.
How simple, the black ants' insistence
my house is permeable.
How dull-witted my annoyance.

Meanwhile, my brain lies on the desk
like a paperweight.
Let it hold things down in there,
as it likes to do.
Out here the body is devoted
only to its desire.

At the foot of the cedar
an anklet of blooming salal dances.
Robins, red-winged blackbirds, rufus-sided towhees
orchestrate my senses into a single instrument.
While the secret ones,
perched in the sombrous woods of my chest,
play their hidden music.

Though I have lived in exile for thirty years,
I am led through a gauntlet of caresses,
become a canal for the memory of moisture.
I am not an orphan, they remind me,

tracing my lineage on my palm then pointing to bark.
Though I have forgotten them
they've kept my picture on the dresser all these years.
I have no language to offer them
but the one the brain perpetrates as language.
Yet my body, my peasant body, surrenders faithfully
to the wordless love of the grasses.

The Garden

*What have you done with the garden
entrusted to you?*
—Antonio Machado

1.

When I call home to check my mail,
she tells me the latest word from the world is
No, jagged as a torn envelope. But

she's been sawing up wooden panels
on which she'll paint icons of our English setter,
our yellow-nape parrot, our two cats,
each with the neighboring hill as a backdrop,
like a medieval landscape. She admits

she suddenly missed me today in the market,
picking out unblemished red potatoes
and pristine ears of corn, missing the way
I check her bags, return the gouged and wormy ones
to the bin. "Oh, you only miss me
in supermarkets," I say. She insists

we've turned a corner. When I leave town now,
she confesses, she lives like a teenage boy
for just a couple of days. She loves our simple life:
the way we cook together, talk in bed
late into the night. Apples are falling

from our tree faster than she can eat
or give them away, so she's blanching
and freezing them for later.

Tomatoes are sacrificing themselves
on the altar of her mayonnaise-laden sandwiches.
Acorn squash fill like bellies,
but sow bugs have become squatters on the peppers.

2.

Late that night, still snared in the sticky net
of sleep, I surface to remember my dreams:
    All night I search the plum-dark city
    for a coffee shop that will let me
    set up my portable Smith-Corona.
    "It's the size and color
    of a thick slice of bread," I offer
    in my defense. All night
    my sleep is trampled
    by tiny black tanks.

I turn on a lamp. Through my reflection
the red geranium blooms out of a hole
in the patio, the asparagus fern launches
another monstrous shoot, the green note
of morning plays the leaves of the ginger,
now that I've trimmed back the holly
that was darkening the yard.
Back along the perimeter fence the bougainvillea dangles
bursts of coral at the tips of spider legs, finally,
after eight barren years. Last year

you could not have convinced me
I would fall in love again.
My garden lay abandoned in yellow weeds.
Is this what love is? Bending the will

all winter and spring, pulling at the ground?
Clearing once more the path between fruit trees?
Watering the desert? What faith

moved me to haul out the remains
of the old bench, buy another, sturdier one
to place at the secluded spot
behind the garage wall
where I set up the typewriter
to record the progress and settle in
to see what happens next?

Risotto Ariosto

Sauté a medium-sized onion, finely
chopped, in two ounces of butter until
it is pliant, translucent. It's tricky,

this dish, like verse, so don't overfill
the pan since arborio grows. The key
is fluid, poured by cups and brought to boil

gently, then stirred like passions unexpressed.
More broth softens the stubborn pearls. Add wine. Test.

What the Water Gave Me

For Leonard Sanazaro

THE WATERFALL

Thunderous locomotion, a roar, rhythmic
clack of freight car, freight car, freight car.
Visible wind on granite face, Saran wrap
hair shaping/reshaping off the forehead.
Let go the head, that cave
from which all bats have flown anyway.
What of the body, then? A black beetle
advances like ancient machinery. The left hand
sweeps it away without curiosity.
So thirsty.

USURPED CORRIDOR

Barely daybreak, a scratching on a post
outside the window. Steller's jay visitation:
blue body bristles, black crest tilts,
hematite eye penetrates sleep.
Unruly cowlick echoes one on the man,
seven and seventy, who stumbles into morning's kitchen—
white robe, swollen eyes—seeking water:
baptismal, disastrous, transformative.

TRANSPARENT BONDAGE

Watery will reshapes history, obliterates evidence,
gets its own way. Riverlike muscle,
a man who has beaten a woman,
carves a course through the brain
to arrive there quicker next time.

PASTORAL

Len is sacked out on a recline-o-rock,
taffy-twist of current at his feet.
Near the falls, that mirror force,
he surrenders. His pale body's a gentle landscape.
On the trail he says, "I don't know whether
Arinata Fuccelli is a flower or a soprano."
Log downstream: lost canoe? silver slipper?

ADVANCING THE PLOT

Stick washes up at my feet.
I toss it into the frantic whiteness,
praying it forward, down, toward calm.
No such luck. Begins again its antigravity
salmon journey. Again I aim, again
it boomerangs. *Let it go, let it go, go, go,*
the water angel says.

Inspiration

For Alix

1.

Does a parrot wait to be invited
before she cracks open the almond?
She is not held back by manners or beliefs.
She has only her passion
for what's beneath the hard shell.
Her pointy gaze as she works
is evidence of her devotion.

2.

And no amount of flattery,
no hyperbole—which isn't
hyperbole at all but the truth
about how stunning she is
in that dollop of sunshine
just now spooned from heaven
into the window where she perches
in the limelight, no, *is* the limelight,
a bloom of iridescent green
firing from within like a synapse—
can pull her attention
away from the honeymoon
of her charcoal beak coaxing
the sweet flesh from the almond
at last.

Backyard Opera

For Juney

I march through the yard with a hard eye,
yanking weeds, asserting a path,
incensed by the relentless advance
of honeysuckle and morning glory vines
weaving under everything like an insidious subtext,
determined to have their loopy, insensible say
even as I slash them back, seeking their polyphonous source,
my finite gestures meaning nothing to them,
as they know I will tire, drift back into the house
and forget our duet for days, even weeks,
letting them spin their tales, full of plot twists,
almost orchestrating my little bench into their melody,
so that when I finally cut back a spot and sit,
and the chimes pick up a phrase of wind,
it becomes clear I am just a half note of silence,
a pause in the longer song.

The Powerful Green Hill

And then I arrived at the powerful green hill.
—Muriel Rukeyser

It's spring again,
and the rusted-metal Mayan goddess
tiptoes through the backyard
tattooed with leaf shadows
like a dancer in a lace body stocking.

Narcissus extend tiny hands
in papery gloves, and a bee
lolls inside a pink rabbit-ear camellia
like a wealthy citizen on satin sheets
late in the morning.

The red garden chair
mouths light into words
and only asks
that we sit still
long enough to decipher them.

What would happen
if we made it easier
for what's trying to reveal itself
to make contact?
Like that hill across there:

blushing green with all it wants to say.
What would happen if we turned
every window to face it, until its green
became the secret room
at the center of our house?

What if we didn't shut out the world's sensations,
its incessant practical jokes?
Let the wind sneak in,
let the rain find a hairline crack
and track wet prints across the floor.

What if we consented to get off
the last of the wooden roller coasters,
let go of the edgy exhilaration
as it shakes and rattles and lifts from its track?
What if we abandoned its finely orchestrated terror?

It's spring, remember? Camphor trees
look like brains lit up with a brilliant idea.
Listen, something is calling.

Jacaranda

The sun comes through the front window,
sits on the little wrought-iron bench
covered in burnt-sugar sculptured velvet,

and I'm old enough to know it will sit like this
only once.
      In the darkened living room my face shines

from the reflection off the fabric and a book that's there—
a monograph on early California plein air painting—
but the amber light seems to flow from me instead,

the way the jacaranda this time of year
blooms so furiously it creates a double on the pavement,
a girl in a summer dress who has walked away from the rest,

stands foot-to-foot with the other girl
upside down in the lake, and it's hard to tell at first
which way is up, which is the true one, which

tossed the violet blossoms—that hover, like confetti,
             only briefly, just this once,
         before they drop—

and which girl perishes, which remains.

The Invisible Body

Regla lesbia: *Flexible rule that may be adjusted to any body to be measured.* Compare regla fija: *standard.*
— *The Velázquez Dictionary*

I.

In the garden, it's there. Even when you're inside you feel it,
as though it were you standing naked among the weeds,

the tips of the bougainvillea bursting into flame, your nipples
ruffled like the skin of a lake by a breeze.

You worship the invisible body like an old-fashioned lover, from afar,
loving the specificity of space between you.

Sometimes at night it stretches out on the empty side
of the bed, stares at you with the length of its invisible surface.

Every contour of your body not filled by you is molded
by the attentiveness of the invisible body, whose breath surrounds
    you.

It's more than prayer it wants—more than language, with its
    conditions.
The invisible body demands you invent new senses to receive it,

new places on your body to marvel at its subtlety,
like the eyes of the deaf percussionist that perceive sound.

II.

The invisible body wants you to become a satellite dish,
tuned to what exists only because your body calls to it.

92

Like the woman who had her kitchen remodeled to make room
for the microwave she'd entered a contest for. Then won.

III.

When asked whether falling in love was about acquisitiveness,
about the ego, the seventy-five-year-old poet

responded that the ego had nothing to do with it;
it was the need for union with the beloved.

Rumi asks, *Who is it we spend our entire lives loving?*

IV.

How, then, do you measure the invisible body,
which resists commitment but is faithful?

Is it clear who the beloved is, when no clear
body exists that can be measured against a standard?

V.

The invisible body sometimes acquires a body—it's so convincing,
it takes you a while to figure out it's really the invisible body.

Like someone who has been reading your journal,
it has decoded from your petty, daily complaints the open sesame

that slides the stone from the hidden cave's opening
and cleans you out while you sleep, leaving a sarcastic note.

It wants you to know it was doing you a favor, besides,
how else did you think you'd discover the cave's precise location?

When Aphrodite sharpens you, you sacrifice a little of yourself, willingly, as a knife does, so that you may become better at it.

VI.

This is the point at which the invisible body speaks
in italics, the Ouija board of poetry.

In my mind, says the invisible body, *that time capsule shuttling through space, I hold, in all the languages of the world,*

*your love, rushed like holographic platters to a table,
steaming into the future long after you've ceased to shine,*

*the silver faces of your beloved bobbing out of the darkness,
the black velvet pillow of your life on which you offer them for view.*

VII.

The invisible body is created out of your longing, your longing
compressing invisible molecules together into an absence you
    recognize.

That is the way one blind man sees the world—after the fact,
in photographs he took, once he had passed through it.